MW01140286

Beverlee was raised on a small farm in Washington where she cared for the family pigs, chickens, and the pet cow. It bothered her that Molly and Dolly felt depressed during the heavy rains, and Lady felt sad when she was separated from her herd. Realizing that animals feel emotions like humans do, she vowed she'd do something with her life to help animals. Beverlee had a successful career working as a lobbyist for national animal organizations and changing laws to better protect animals. She currently lives on a large strawberry ranch and operates Crops and Critters, an animal rescue facility where tours are held for school children.

"I noticed that children with special needs would stand away from their group and gravitate to the special needs animals like Tiny Timm. This book is for them."

A True Story Of Tiny Timm

A Little Bunny Who Made Friends
and Brought Joy to Everyone

Beverlee McGrath

AUSTIN MACAULEY PUBLISHERS™
LONDON • CAMBRIDGE • NEW YORK • SHARJAH

Ordering Information
Quantity sales: Special discounts are available on quantity purchases by corporations, associations, and others. For details, contact the publisher at the address below.

Publisher's Cataloging-in-Publication data
McGrath, Beverlee
A True Story Of Tiny Timm

ISBN 9781685628444 (Paperback)
ISBN 9781685628451 (Hardback)
ISBN 9781685628475 (ePub e-book)

Library of Congress Control Number: 2023910050

www.austinmacauley.com/us

First Published 2022
Austin Macauley Publishers LLC
40 Wall Street, 33rd Floor, Suite 3302
New York, NY 10005
USA

mail-usa@austinmacauley.com
+1 (646) 5125767

Dedicated to all of the children with special needs that bonded with Tiny Timm and love him.

My daughter, Bridget, who inspired me to write the book, and her assistance.

To Ray Christian who took all of the photographs of Tiny Timm.

A True Story of Tiny Timm, a Little Bunny That Was Born with Legs That Never Worked

He Can't Hop, But He Never Gives Up, and He Loves Every Living Creature.
He Also Loves Hugs and Cheerios

By Beverlee Mcgrath (With a Little Help from Her Daughter, Bridget Mcgrath)

I Live in a Big House with Mommy, My Brother Tunnel, and My Brothers and Sisters. I Have Lots of Friends, Too. and by the Way, My Human Mommy Lives There Too.

I Have So Much to Do Today! Wanna Come Along?
Let's Go!

I Wake Up in the Morning and My Brother, Tunnel, Licks My Face and Ears Before Breakfast. Tunnel Has Always Taken Care of Me. He Taught Me How to Eat and Scurry Around on My Knees, Since I Can't Hop Like Other Bunnies.

Mommy Was Too Busy with All of My Brothers and Sisters, So Tunnel Raised Me. I Love Him Best.

I Don't Wear a Diaper, But I Need to Have Bath Time First Thing in the Morning, so I Start My Day Dapper Clean.

I'm So Lucky to Have So Many Friends like Cooper Kitty. He Watches Me Have My Bath, But He Doesn't Like to Get Wet, So He Just Watches. Mommy Told Me and Tunnel We Have to Eat the Food Human Mommy Gives Us Because It Will Make Us Strong.

I'll Share Some with Cooper Because Cooper Shares with Me.

Sweetie, My Doggy Friend, Sniffs Me to See If I'm Okay. She Really Worries About Me. She Whines and Chuffs the Whole Time I'm in the Bath.

After Bath-time, She Has to Give Me a Big Fat Slobbery Kiss to Let Me Know How Happy She Is That I Made It

Through Bath-time. I Could Do Without Those Big Fat Slobbery Doggy Kisses, But I Don't Want to Hurt Her Feelings, So I Don't Tell Her.

Yay, Bath Time Is Over.
Time to Play!

This Is the Best Time of Day, When We All Play Together!
I Have Special Needs and I'm Able to Share Love and Live
a Happy Full Life. Even Though I'm Different, My Brothers,
Sisters and Friends Love and Accept Me for Who I Am.

Sometimes Caboodle Kitty Comes to Visit Tunnel and Me. She Always Smells Good. The Animal Angel Gave Her Soft Fur Like Tunnel.

When the Weather Is Really Nice, We Get to Play Outside.
We All Go to the Village.

This Is My House in the Village. I Share It with Mommy and Tunnel.

Look How Big I Look in My House!

My Other Friends Live Close to the Village. This Is Alex, the Alpaca. Alex and I like to Talk About Butterflies.

"A Butterfly Landed on My Ear This Morning. I Wanted to Ask Her What She Was Doing But My Ear Flicked and She Flew Away Before I Could Ask," Said Alex.

"I Think I Might Be Too Little for the Butterflies to Land on Me," I Said. "But I Watch Them Fly Around Up High in the Village All the Time."

I Like to Watch the Skunks Come Up on the Porch for Dinner. They Eat All of Our Leftovers and They Really Love My Leftover Cheerios.

Then There's Greg, The Goat. Greg and I like to Talk About Moths. Greg likes to Try to Catch Them.

"Have You Ever Actually Caught One?" I Ask.
"One Time I Did. I Was Amazingly Fast
That Day," Greg Told Me.
"What Was It Like?" I Asked Greg.
"Powdery," Greg Wisely Told Me.

When We Went Trick-Or-Treating Last Halloween, Greg Was Supposed to Go As a Reindeer, But He Was Grumpy and Refused to Wear His Hat and Antlers, So He Was Just in a Pink Jumper.

Sweetie Went As a Bumblebee and I Went As a Flower.
Only Two People Gave Me Carrots.

This Is Franklin. Franklin Talks a Lot and He Does Special Tricks for the School Children When They Come to Visit Us.

"The Squirrels Were at It Again Today!" Franklin Announced.
"Chattering Too Loudly and Disturbing Your Nap?" I Asked.
"No, Grabbing the Nuts, Then Burying the Nuts. Grabbing the Nuts, Then Burying the Nuts. Over and Over. Why Do They Do That?" Franklin Asked.
"Maybe They're Saving for a Rainy Day," I Suggested. Although I've Wondered Why They Do That, Too.

This Is Precious. She's Tiny, Like Me. My Human Mommy Named Her Just Right, Don't You Think?

Precious Likes to Tell Me How Warm and Cozy She Is in Her Sweater and How She Gets Special Human Mommy Time Inside the House.

"*Guess What?*" Precious Says. "*It's Dinner Time!*" She Announced Before I Could Guess. Precious Really Likes Dinner Time.

We Eat Together As One Big Family. But the Guinea Pigs Eat Special Guinea Pig Pellets That Have Vitamin C in Them. I Don't Like Their Pellets.

My Brothers and Sisters and I Have Our Very Own Rabbit Pellets, But We All Love Hay! We Also Love Kale, Cilantro and Carrots.

After Dinner, We All Start To Get Very Sleepy.

Time for Bed!

Sweetie Tells Me It's Bedtime and She Wants To Give Me Another Slobbery Doggy Kiss Goodnight.

"But if You Kiss Me Goodnight, You'll Get My Pajama Sweater All Wet," I Say.
I Think It Worked.

If I Stand Very Still While My Human Mommy Puts on My Favorite Pajama Sweater, I Get a Bedtime Story. Human Mommy Tells Good Stories.

I Like My Sweater Because It Keeps Me Warm and Cozy. My Human Mommy Takes Good Care of Me.

Tonight I'm Going to Dream About the Squirrels Burying Their Nuts and Catching Moths.

Maybe a Butterfly Will Land on My Head Tomorrow. Wouldn't That Be Something?! Tomorrow Is Going to Be An Amazing Day!

Thank You For Visiting Me and Meeting My Family and Friends. Next Visit I'll Show You the Great Big Horses That Sound like Thunder When They Walk!
Tiny Timm, Along with His Family and Friends, Lives on a Strawberry Ranch on Oxnard, California.

THE END